Dying to Live

PART I SERIES

"Messages Beyond"

By
Charlene Elizabeth Emeterio,
LCSW-R, CCT, CCTP, BCD, Ph.D.

Balboa Press books may be ordered through booksellers or by contacting:

Balboa Press
A Division of Hay House
1663 Liberty Drive
Bloomington, IN 47403
www.balboapress.com
844-682-1282

Because of the dynamic nature of the Internet, any web addresses or links contained in this book may have changed since publication and may no longer be valid. The views expressed in this work are solely those of the author and do not necessarily reflect the views of the publisher, and the publisher hereby disclaims any responsibility for them.

Any people depicted in stock imagery provided by Getty Images are models, and such images are being used for illustrative purposes only. Certain stock imagery © Getty Images.

ISBN: 978-1-9822-6470-3 (sc)
ISBN: 978-1-9822-6471-0 (e)

Print information available on the last page.

Balboa Press rev. date: 05/10/2021

BALBOA.PRESS
A DIVISION OF HAY HOUSE

Contents

INTRODUCTION

There is no such thing as a coincidence. It was meant for you to read this book. You will gain something from it since you have an open mind. "Dying to Live" is the name of this book because we are here temporarily and eventually we return to our real home called Heaven. At some time determined by our Lord, our physical bodies die and become spirit bodies. I have no fear of this because there is another world close by known as our real home. My parents crossed over and sent me messages about this. This is where all our loved ones continue living. The true stories are a combination of "Messages Beyond" with faith and eternal love.

This book is dedicated to my dear beloved parents Joseph and Lois Emeterio. Both of my parents were gifts and special blessings to me. As a licensed psychotherapist, I know that there are people who have never known this kind of love from their parents. I can only have faith that there are other people in their life where love has been experienced. Love is what life is really all about. As I stated at my father's funeral, if I could only duplicate my father for all the abused children in this world, it would be a better world full of kindness. This is the first series of books about their messages. The first part is about my mother's illness and my father crossing over with the messages he starts to send.

The second part is about my mother's story and the messages. As my parents reunite, then even more powerful messages begin to come. The messages can help us keep our loving new spiritual relationship with our loved ones. It is an honor to share these messages with you in an effort to bring you a new kind of faith because we will all face the challenges of losing a loved one.

PREFACE

My father returned home to Heaven on 2/28/11 and my mother on 8/7/11. My grief is complicated with two special people leaving my life so close together. Complicated in the respect of a different grief cycle and we do not expect to lose two people at the same time that mean everything to us. We were very close and my parents were everything to me. My father played many important roles in my life. He was my best friend, business partner and part of my collective soul. It is a bond of love that carries on in many ways. My father leaving was so unexpected because he was always so healthy and my mother was the one who had been ill. I now know that my father had to leave before my mother to help her over to the astral plane called Heaven.

I remember a priest saying to me, what were the chances of both of your parents going to Florida and meeting each other? He went on to say it was divine intervention. It was indeed divine intervention and meant for my parents to meet and to be with each other for eternity. There is a special plan for all of us. While there are choices, some things are just meant to happen and are actually already planned. You see, my mother was from Kentucky and on vacation in Miami, Florida. My father was from upstate New York and went to try out for professional baseball in Miami, Florida. They met on Miami Beach, married and stayed there. I came along later as described by mom as the miracle baby.

This book was especially written to help others who are on a journey of grief. It is a continued journey about eternal love. Love is what life and Heaven are all about. May your visions and hearts be open even more after spending some time with me on this journey. Please understand that the sharing of the messages that continue are all being written to help others and to give faith in our world where many people need this. The veil has become thinner and we can ask to receive messages from our loved ones. Just keep an open mind and heart as you read this book.

I want to thank each and every person for taking time to join me on my journey to eternal love. May God Bless and bring peace within your heart. May these writings bring you comfort during your journey called life on earth.

ACKNOWLEDGMENTS:

First, thank you Lord for guiding me through this journey called life on earth. Special appreciation for my beloved parents who are now my guardian angels guiding me from another dimension called Heaven. I also want to thank my mother for the gift of writing poetry and guiding me through some of the poems written in this book.

Thanks to all the clients who chose to come to me during their journey of grief. I so appreciate all the clients sent to me during this journey of grief...especially all the beautiful children and their families.

Many thanks to Don Greico for the Myrtle Beach golfing pictures given to my father. My father enjoyed this special friendship and companionship for many years.

Thanks to Dave Roberts, my colleague at Sacred Heart Healing Center and friend for assisting with the submitting of the photographs portrayed in this book. Your support and patience was greatly appreciated.

SPECIAL NOTATIONS:

All of the poetry in this book is written by the author. Most of the poems were written in a trance like state called automatic writing. Most of the photographs were taken by the author or family member.

"Messages Beyond"

Today I heard a special song from my dear dad,

Yesterday I saw the beautiful purple petunias that appeared

In a flash from my dear mother and not too long ago

There was two clouds shaped like hearts as I drove home

from the cemetery. Life exists on the astral plane. As we find peace in

knowing that love is eternal and our loved ones have only traveled,

death does not even exist.

About three and half years prior to my mother becoming ill, she found a small bump towards the side of her head. I remember my mother going to the doctor to get this checked out a couple of different times. She kept saying "I sure hope they are right about nothing being wrong. I don't know about this."

Within a few short months, I noticed when my mother moved her hair to the side that the small bump grew larger to the size of about a lemon. My father was concerned about all this and we told my mother that she must go back and request some medical scans. She did do this and this is when the rapid growing tumor was discovered. Major brain surgery was the only option at this point because the tumor had grown too large in size. The good news was that it was benign. There was no family history of any brain tumors. I sometimes have wondered if it had to do with toxins and side effects of medications. Anyway, once my mother was diagnosed with this, she had major brain surgery. She went through rehabilitation and was able to get back to her normal functioning which was amazing for her age. My mother eventually got to a point where she was able to do things she did before. There was some changes with my mother but she was able to get back to her normal routine eventually. She enjoyed more time here with us. My mother had survived a very serious major brain operation and with some follow-up surgery as well as at least two gamma knife perfexion treatments. During this process, she had many different kinds of magnetic resonance imaging (MRI) to monitor the tumor. Some were painful with injections. My father took good care of her and was her primary caregiver. He was so kind and gentle with her. My mother got back to enjoying activities and my parents were able to go out again. My father handled the follow–up doctor appointments and making sure my mother ate healthy. He was very attentive and nurturing in all ways.

During my mother's time with all of this, many things transpired. My mother went through a lot. She had the top of her head shaved for the surgery and lost her hair with the follow-up treatments. The first surgery was delayed because of the blood results but they had already shaved her head. So, my mother had to go home like this and wait at least two more weeks. Then she was admitted after I wrote a letter about my concerns and spent quite some time being prepared for surgery including two blood transfusions and several platelets. She went through intensive rehabilitation and outpatient therapy. She always had so much strength and faith. I remember praying for her with my father in the waiting room. When I looked up, there was a picture of Christ looking at me. This was a very risky operation with my mother's medical history. However, I felt my mother would survive this. I would begin to get messages that would validate this. The first room she had was right near a cross. I looked out the window to see that a cross was facing her window from the outside. I remember receiving in the mail a special prayer right before her surgery which I held on to for prayers. These messages and synchronized events would give me continued faith.

There was some humor to be found in all of this. While my mother was in intensive care, the nurses asked me why she kept counting numbers. They thought that maybe she was counting her pills. I listened one day while she was in intensive care. She was counting but not pills. I could tell that she was betting horses. My mother loved the horses and I could tell by the way she was counting. Another sign that my mother was going to be alright. Shortly after speaking with the nurses about the numbers, my mother was moved out of intensive care. Eventually she was transferred to intensive rehabilitation and then acute care rehabilitation. My father and I visited every day. My mother was learning to walk and talk again. It was like my mother had to start learning to think and talk all over. We showed her pictures and words all the time. We knew my mom was getting better when she started to say certain things like "Where is the good food?" Another really humorous time was when I took her to play bingo and my mother covered the entire card and yelled out "Bingo." Covering the whole card paid only a dollar. When my mother found this out, she replied "What can I get with this?" If you knew my mother, she usually won big money and couldn't believe it was only a dollar. I knew she was getting back to her old self.

During this time on the rehabilitation unit, I also took my mom for a ride in the wheelchair to get her out of the room for awhile. There were several older people sitting in the hallway on this residential unit next to where she was staying. Her reply was "They are all old and sleeping, this isn't for me." Well, my mom was close to their ages but didn't see herself the same way because she has always been very active. Also, my mom always looked younger for her age. Once again, mom was getting back to herself. Remember my mother had major brain surgery. Her speech was a little slow but her thinking was just incredible for just having major brain surgery. I also remember taking that dollar she won and buying her an ice ream. Of course, even the ice cream was more then a dollar.

While in the rehabilitation unit, I brought in some scarfs to match her outfits. She received so many complements on them. The scarfs covered up her baldness on top of her head; while giving her hair time to grow back. Later, a wig was ordered for her to wear when she got discharged from treatment. Her hair grew back quickly and more thick. We got some outpatient services for my mother. My father would be there when they came to the house. The physical therapy seem to help a lot. The lady who came was very militant like as described by my mother. My mother did those exercises every day. She was determined to get better. The speech therapist did not work out very well. There were some sessions but my mother didn't want to continue. She felt it was too "baby like." It took some time but my mother started to get her speech back and even balancing the check book. It appeared that watching television, reading, and speaking with my father seem to help the most. My mother was full of motivation, strength, and love. My father was full of love and compassion. They were eventually like two kids in love again.

It all started a little before the fall of 2011 with my father. I noticed my father not being himself. He was having problems with a tooth. There was no infection but there was bone loss. Time passed and my father continued to have problems. He kept going back and finally I told my father that he needed a referral to a specialist. We went to see the specialist about three times total. I will never forget the biopsy report and when my father was given the news of early stages of cancer. It was so devastating to hear this shocking news. It is still so painful to even put this into words. I was with my father and told him that we would fight this.

My father fought so hard and there was so much pain. To this day, there is no real explanation as to how my father got cancer of the jaw. He was always in good health and did not drink/smoke. He was emotionally, mentally, and very physically fit. He played every sport and was so athletic all his life. When he retired from the state, my father would laugh and say "I just play golf now." He played with people a lot younger than himself and right up until the diagnosis. My father usually walked the golf course. He was so up to date on healthy living too. He grew his own garden and ate plenty of vegetables.

So, what went wrong? I believe trauma from the tooth. The tooth was never pulled and one day it just came out in his sleep.

Several months after this, he started to have a lot of pain. This is when the cancer was found. It is possible that trauma can activate cancer cells. So we thought this was early stages of cancer but when we finally got the appointment to see the surgeon, it was stage four cancer. My father had to get a major 10 hour surgery to remove the cancer. It would be 18 hours if bone was taken from his leg to replace the jaw. We decided to start with the 10 hour surgical procedure and perhaps later getting the bone procedure done.

While waiting for the surgery, the tumor got bigger and I could see a tumor forming in his chin but this was benign. The pain was so unbearable for my father. The pain medication helped to some extent but as it grew during the end of October, the pain was incredible. It was so difficult watching my father suffer. I got the appointment moved up but not soon enough because it had grown. My father finally got the surgery and did well. I remember wearing his golf hat all the way home and being so thankful for this. I drove the 60 minute drive everyday until he was discharged. He came home in time for Thanksgiving but could not eat any food. This was the sad part and he had to remain on the feeding tube temporarily. My mother was quite sick herself and worried about him.

My father was home briefly and having problems. I was going to call an ambulance and have him transported back to the hospital but decided to take him myself. He was able to get dressed and walk. However, he was not doing well at all. It was a stormy snowy day. My father had gotten off balance and fell. Fortunately, I caught him in time. We left for the hospital and went through the emergency room. He was admitted and diagnosed with pneumonia. My father survived the pneumonia after almost a three week battle. He was then transferred to a rehabilitation unit where he would learn to speak and walk again. They had just started closing down the intensive care unit. As a result, he went to the acute care unit for rehabilitation. At first, he thrived and was walking faster than the nurses. He told me that the walker should go to somebody who really needs it.

He started speaking again and worked so hard progressing with this. The walking came easy to my father because of his athletic background. He advanced so quickly. He came home for Christmas and New Year's Day. He was having some minor pain in his chin that got worse. We were told by the doctor who did the follow-up how common pain in the chin was with this surgical procedure. However, the pain in the chin continued to get worse. I made many phone calls about this and we went for a scan. We were told at the time that there was an infection, fluid, or the cancer was returning. The surgeon claimed that he was 99% sure that the cancer had returned and if this was true, he did not know how long my father would live. He said this in front of my father and we could not wait to leave this office. I decided to have a biopsy at the rehabilitation hospital setting. The results were benign and the pus that started to come out of the chin was drained.

Shortly after this, my father is sent for a blood transfusion. I found this out when he was not in his room and I quickly left to be with him. My father was not doing well at all. They were treating him for the infection and giving him a blood transfusion. There was a wait because the blood transfusion identification bracelet was lost. Once the blood transfusion started my father eventually seem uncomfortable. I kept calling the nurse on duty. He also started having some breathing problems. At one point he looked at me as though he wasn't himself and just like he had seen something. He kept trying to tell me something but I didn't know what was going on. There seem to be a lot of fluids building up and his blood pressure increased significantly. The blood pressures started bouncing all over the place. While he did stabilize, my father was not himself. He went from the blood transfusion unit to the rehabilitation unit. Because of what they gave him, he was up all night in the bathroom. As a result of this, he was not able to get the sleep he needed.

Right before all of this happened, I kept advocating for blood testing to see if there was an infection. This was not done until I took my father to see a cancer radiologist across the street. Then the blood work was done and my father did in fact have an infection. He also needed a blood transfusion after having the tumor removed from his chin. By this time, my father had a spreading infection. His neck was red and turned purple. The infection was causing breathing problems. The treatment for the infection had come too late. My father was rushed to the emergency room and went into heart failure.

While in the emergency room, my father at one point kept looking up at the ceiling as if he was seeing things. Then he asked me where my mother was at. My cousin and I kept a close eye on him until a room on the medical floor opened up even though I felt my father should of been admitted to the intensive care unit for close monitoring at this point. He was finally admitted to the medical floor on the heart unit.

My father was having a hard time talking because of the congestion. He gestured to me to take the boot off his leg after he knocked the other one off. The nurse told me it was alright so I gladly tossed it. He went right to sleep. Visiting hours were over by the time he was admitted. So, I told my father while he was sleeping, how much I loved him and would be back tomorrow. At this point, he was sound asleep and I did not want to wake him.

"Long days and nights"

The pain strikes

Crying out for help

Infection strikes

Long days and nights

The infection came

And put dad to rest

Long days and nights

Crying alone into the nights

Darkness came

Tears remain.

At about 2:30 am, I could not sleep and felt as though my father was calling me. I called the hospital and asked the night nurse to check on my father. The nurse mentioned just being in there and how my father was trying to talk. However, he could not understand my father. I told the nurse that there was a writing board by his bedside to use and to please let me know my father's status soon. The nurse indicated that he would go back again to check on my father. About 4:20 am, I got the worst call of my life. They had been doing cardiopulmonary resuscitation on my father when he died. I rushed to the hospital and called my cousin who came too.

The attending night nurse told me that he went to check and found my father struggling. Words can't even explain how I felt. My life had changed forever and now I had to tell my mother who was not doing well. I believe my mother already had an idea when I rushed out of the house to leave for the hospital. I cried so much that a river could of flowed through my parents' house. From this day on, my mother would begin to explain my tears to people when I tried talking about my father. Even during her illness she was able to be so supportive to me in these difficult emotional moments.

"Shattered Pieces Of My Heart"

Along the path

All alone

Piece by piece

All around

"Shattered Pieces One By One…"

Day by day

Piece by piece

Along the path

All alone

"Shattered Pieces Of My Heart"

Along the path

Remain alone.

I have experienced many different kinds of losses. There were losses in death too but my father's death changed me forever. The only way to describe this was like the largest ocean wave I had ever encountered came out of no where knocking me over completely. I remember talking about my sadness and grief with others. I certainly received plenty of warm hearted and well intended comments. However, most it was very contradictory. For example, I recall one person saying stay busy and another person saying to get plenty of rest. I continue to grieve in my own way. I had to find a way to get through this and continue to take care of my mother who really needed me. When I got up from feeling like a tidal wave had knocked me over, I felt totally lost. This is when the Lord came and carried me.

My mother barely made it to the funeral. I felt my father's presence there. I remember placing my father's golf hat in the casket and an article about my dog, Reiki's healing abilities. This was the same golf hat I wore after his successful surgery. I remember seeing two young cousins trying to touch my father and how they kept looking at him. I was so numb and sick. Nothing really mattered to me. I was still in shock of everything that had transpired and concerned about my mother. They had the veterans tribute at the chapel which was beautiful despite the very cold and snowy weather. The flowers were all so beautiful and the golf ball arrangement was touching. There were many people at the wake and family at the chapel despite the snow storm.

My mother and I decided to get some dinner and stop at the store after the funeral. I went in the store with my mom and she wanted a little time to look around. So, I hesitantly left to go home with the flower arrangements to drop them off. I came right back to the store and pulled up to get my mother but she was not there. I felt this really uncomfortable feeling and then heard this telepathic message from my father saying "Go in the store now." Then I heard the fire department and ambulance. I ran in right behind the firemen. I followed them knowing that something had happened to my mother. She was laying flat down in the check out lane on the floor with her eyes closed. My mother soon opened her eyes and said "I am alright." She apparently knew she was going to fall and hung on to the side of the lane and fell to her side. After my mom fell, she laid down because there was no way to get back up. Her legs had given out but did not hit her head as suspected. The medical staff thought she was alright and my mother did not want to go to the hospital. So, we left and went home. From this time on, I knew something else was wrong with my mother.

One day after my father's crossing to Heaven, I was sitting in the living room giving my mother her insulin. My mother hears me talking out loud prior to entering. She wants to know who I am speaking to. I explain that I am speaking with my father. She says "Can he really hear you?" I explain to her that I believe so. So, my mother says "Well, hear this." She starts talking to him too. Then I ask my mother to send me a beautiful butterfly if she crosses over before me. She tells me that she will pour all kinds of things down for me. My mother always had a wonderful sense of humor. I tell her to send me the most beautiful butterfly to let me know she has transformed to the spirit body. My mother just smiles and says "Oh, I will."

While I knew that something else could be going on with my mother, I did not know that she would soon cross over too. We were planning on my mother moving over to my house. The process of this had started and my mother was feeling more comfortable with the idea. After all, she did not need to be alone in a house by herself. It just made more sense to transition to my house and making a couple of rooms similar to hers. She went through her closet and decided what she wanted to donate. My mom planned on taking only what she really wanted to keep.

On the weekend of July 4th 2011, this would all turn in a different direction. I had been taking my mom for lymphedema treatments on her legs. It had taken awhile to get in for these treatments. It seem like the treatments were working again but at one point I realized that there was something else happening. I took my mom to the urgent care where she was getting the lymphedema treatments. We were there most of the day. She was not admitted but instead was set up to see her primary doctor the next day. They did many tests while at urgent care. The doctors indicated that something was going on causing the fluids building up. The primary doctor increased the medication but this was not enough. So, on the 4th of July, I called the primary doctor and told him I was going to admit my mother to the hospital for further examination. At first, they thought it was a bleeding ulcer and they treated this. After further testing, the real problems were found. My mother had a tumor on her liver that was large. The tumor was causing her breathing problems. She was in intensive care for three weeks and the regular hospital unit for at least two weeks. She was on a bypass machine and was able to come off this several times. However, she would have to go back on it because the fluids continued to increase due to the tumor.

I prayed every day by her bedside for hours knowing a miracle was needed. At one point, my mother tells me not to leave. She says "Don't go, good news is coming." This happened a couple of times. She would seem disappointed when I had to leave and sometimes I would stay longer. On July 28, the rehabilitation people came in and she got halfway out of bed saying "That's my daughter, it's her birthday." My mom had several decent days before this happened. She came off the machine for longer periods of time. However, the next day after my birthday, my mother started to slip away. She eventually went into a coma state. I had to make some decisions. I felt a lot of pressure at one point from the hospital staff. I had decided on certain things but I put everything into the Lord's hands. I got a beautiful miracle when my mother was able to spend the day with me on my birthday. It was the best gift ever. I would not take her medications away even though she was in a coma. Before my mother went into a coma, she never complained of pain. However, I agreed to morphine the last day when her body was shutting down. I really felt at this point that her soul went to Heaven but the attending physician told me she was suffering.

I had left the room with my cousin debating this pressure of taking the medicines away with my cousin. It didn't make sense to do this. It was in the Lord's hands. I returned to the room and spent my last few minutes with my mother. My mother decided to leave with the Lord. Her face glowed and her skin was beautiful. I later realized that the good news my mother was talking about had to do with seeing my father again. I know she didn't want me to leave those few times because the angels told her that my father was coming. She thought that I would see him too. It was a difficult night for me. I had lost my father and now my mother.

My world was so different now. I felt like a orphan at the time in some ways but knew how blessed I was to have my parents for so many years. I was tired and so sick and worn out. My own health was deteriorating. My cousin and I left to get some sleep. The next day my cousin and I meet outside in a picnic area. It was a warm hot humid day and out of the clear blue sky, the most beautiful butterfly started flying around me. Then this cool wind came around me and it was if my mother gave me a hug to let me know that she had made it to Heaven. The cool wind left as quick as it came. I knew in my heart that my mother had been transformed back to her beautiful spirit body. I was remembering our talk after my father died about sending me the most beautiful butterfly if she crossed over before me. This would not be the last time to hear from my mother. She would send many more messages in many different ways.

My journey with grief continued. I was grieving my father and now my mother. I thought to myself, how will I ever live my life with so much drastic change all at once. There was so much to handle. It seem like the only real thing that helped was the messages. My spirituality was holding me together. I had lost my whole world now. You see, no matter who you have currently in your life, it just doesn't replace the people who have crossed over. This was certainly true with both of my beloved parents. I didn't of course want to replace them. My whole life connection that I had known since birth was missing in the physical form. While I had traveled and been away at times for years, my parents were always just a phone call, drive, or plane flight away. I just wanted to see, speak and spend time with them. Other people were fine but I just wanted that special time with my parents. I knew, my life had changed forever. I had no control over this. This was something that couldn't be changed. My journey would continue, learning to live without my parents as I knew them physically on earth.

"Soul Journey"

On a journey, heart to heart,

softly my soul speaks.

Close to our heart,

we walk in spirit

to eternal light and love.

There were times when I just wanted to shut the world out completely. I could be angry, depressed or embrace this new life. My parents had already decided that they were going to send messages to me on a regular basis so that I could adjust better. It was just so much all at once and they knew this. So the messages came and I never knew when it would happen. There was excitement with this new relationship. I dearly missed the old relationship but there was a sense of a different kind of closeness. When the messages came, it was the best feeling ever. There was a sense of direct communication with my parents. This continued to help me with this journey called grief. My strength would get better and my faith would grow stronger during this journey. I would do things on my own that I never dreamed any individual person could do under such difficult circumstances. I knew it was the messages that would come and give me faith. It would change death as we know forever for me.

One of the first messages to come after the first butterfly was a vision. One night, I saw an image of an angel on the wall at my parents' house. This was shortly after both of my parents had crossed over. At first, I thought this couldn't be happening. I kept looking at this image. It remained and then followed by the face of Christ. Yes, the face of Christ. It appeared slowly and changed to be bigger like in a white cloud or bubble. I was absolutely amazed. It was like time had stopped and what was a few minutes, seemed longer. I felt so at peace right after this vision. It was a strong message about my dear parents. Later, I told a priest to see what would be said about this. His response was simple. He said "Your parents are in the Lord's Kingdom." This is exactly what I thought as well as feeling like they were now looking over me. To this day, I can still see this vision in my mind.

"Gift of Love"

Give you my friendship

Loyal deep heart full of gold

Give you my love

It's truly the treasure of the heart

Essence of the soul

Walking by your side

Close or far away

Treasure of the soul

It does not see with eyes

The soul feels and just knows

Connecting from the heart and soul

ONE at last

Rest and be assured

HOME at last.

Several months after my mother's crossing, I was sleeping late in the morning. I heard a voice saying "Wake up Charlene." I woke up but nobody was there. I looked around and saw my dog just laying there next to me. As I became wide awake, I heard my mother's voice in the room very clearly. My mother had a very distinct beautiful Kentucky accent and she was talking to my dog, Reiki. My mother loved animals and was buddies with Reiki. My dog spent most days with my mother while I was at work. My mother was talking to my dog like she always did. I said "mom." My mother said to me "Let Reiki outside, she wants out." I just sat there looking at my dog. I was still in a shock like state to some extent. I said "Mom, is that you?" "Are you really here?" Mom says "Let the dog out." Then mom disappears and I let my dog, Reiki outside. Afterwards, there was such a sense of peace and love.

I find this humorous in many ways. So, my mom crosses over and finds a way back to tell me what to do. For sure, I had this new spirit relationship and my mom still had her personality. I have to laugh because my mother was always great at telling me what to do. This stayed with me for days. There was a sense of peace and I was learning to adjust to the new spirit relationship. I would get messages to keep me connected. My relationship had never ended through my parents physical death from earth. It was a whole new relationship that would take some adjusting. My parents came back and were actually teaching me how to talk with them. My parents were letting me know they transitioned to Heaven but were still with me.

I was having some struggles on my path with grief as we all do. The journey can turn from one moment to the next with changing emotions. At times, I felt like not going on with life. On one of these days, I found a quarter with a horse on the back and it said Kentucky. Another message from mom assuring me that she is with me and that all will be well. I would later find two more quarters just like this at a time of struggles on my journey with grief. They were instant messages saying all will work out and we are still here with you. She just loved horses and Kentucky was where she grew up.

"My Old Kentucky Home"

A horse on a quarter once
A horse on a quarter twice
A horse on a quarter three times

All three times mom says a horse
Of course, I am right here
A Kentucky horse of course.

"Signs of Angels"

Sweet fragrances in the air
Signs of numbers everywhere
Butterflies go by
Wings to comfort you
Love to embrace a hug
Whispers of caress and grace
Looking down as coins appear
Pennies, dimes
No fears
Love is everywhere
Warm special smile
Quarters appear from Heaven above
A horse, white feather, red cardinal coming by
A father of love
A chill to embrace
Angels all around
Stars, light, galaxies away
All signs of angels all around this day.

Messages can come in many different ways. You can get them through coins, birds, feathers, electrical devices, music and even people. My mother now starts to talk through clients. A teenager comes to see me through the loss of her mother. This teenager loves horses and starts to work on a farm and establishes this special relationship with a horse. The horse helps her deal with the loss of her mother. She begins to love talking about horses just like my mother. The teen goes on a trip and brings back a stone with a butterfly on it. Another message from my mother letting me know she is still around and has transformed back to a beautiful butterfly.

Dear Teen,

Thank you for the stone with the butterfly.
Your connection is like a message from my
mother who loved horses. Our mothers have
transformed into beautiful butterflies.

One day, I ask my mother to send me a real butterfly right after she crosses to Heaven. I ask her to make sure that this doesn't get missed by me. Several days later, I barely crack the door to get the mail. A large monarch butterfly comes from no where and hits me right in the face. I knew right away, this was my mother's sense of humor. I said out loud, "Yes mom, I got the message for sure. I certainly couldn't miss that message. Thank you dear mother. I know you are laughing." Then telepathic like "How is that for seeing?" I could sense her smile and laughter. I remember how she was going to pour all kinds of things down for me from Heaven.

Another message came in an unusual letter from my mother's sister in Kentucky. She starts talking about how she thinks my mother was in the room watching her. My aunt does not talk this way at all. She goes on to talk about her presence in the room. I knew that my mother was there with her. My aunt was having a very hard time with the news of my mother crossing. I know that my mother would want to check on her. My mother has traveled more than a few times to see her over the years. My parents had tried to get her to visit us and even paid for her plane ticket. However, she never came to visit. My aunt had developed some fears of flying on planes and traveling over the years. My mother over the years, did visit her when she could travel. My aunt was having regrets now with my mother's crossing but my mom would be there to comfort her sister in the new spirit form.

"Crossing Dimensions"

Journey of grief
Earthy life times
Love never dies
Just the relationship
Physical to our souls transformation
Lighter like a feather in the air
Sometimes crossing into higher dimensions
Dreaming...
Perhaps really there
Seeing your angel face again
Smiling away with the brightest glow ever
So incredibly young again
Flying in the galaxy
Taking my hand
Then letting go
Smiling with a glow
Happiness magnified in your bright white light

Sending pure love in a warm glow
Letting me know
You are still around
Waking up, the dream is over
Not at all
Traveled to Heavens dimensions
It's true
We live forever
My soul traveled and discovers pure joy
Knowing you are so free
Like a bird with beautiful wings
Heaven on Earth
Earth to Heaven
Love is the answer
Lessons learned
Our souls live on
In a special place.

I started to get messages that my father was still alive and had transformed to his new home in Heaven. The messages began while my mother was still alive. My first message from my father came in what seemed like dreams but they were much more than this. It was like meeting my father in between planes. My first encounter was a dialogue with my father. He came to tell me not to worry about him. He went from what he looked like in his later years to his younger days of about 29 years of age. He eventually showed me his younger face and his teeth glowed in the most beautiful smile. I was so happy to see this due to the surgery he had while living on earth. In one of these encounters, I asked my father if I would see him again. When he replied no, I cried. My father followed with saying "One more time." I realized that he meant not physically on earth but in our spirit bodies. At one point I took his strong hand and it felt like I was there with him. He eventually let go of my hand to allow me to return. I woke up on the floor with a severely injured knee.

Since this time, I have not had any further dreams quite like this. However, I do continue to get all kinds of messages. I believe that traveling to the other plane stopped because of my knee injury. I had problems getting back into my body and really was not quite myself. At this time, I didn't know how I traveled to the other astral plane but it happened. I am sure that my father was concerned about the injury and this is probably why this travel has not occurred again. I really wanted to go with him too and he knew it was not my time.

Before my father crossed over, I asked him to send me tons of Beatles songs if he crossed over to Heaven before me. I heard tons of Beatles songs everywhere I went. Some very unusual Beatles songs too. I would ask people if it was Beatles mania week or month. It was not of course. I still hear special songs from the Beatles now but it is always when I am having a hard time without his physical presence. It will usually be at least three or four songs in one day. I hear these songs in his car and just about anywhere I go. There is a special song James Taylor wrote that we played a lot when my father was going through speech and physical therapy. This song called "You Got A Friend" comes on at times when something difficult turns out good. For example, after getting everything completed at the bank regarding both estates, this song came on in a grocery store. I knew my father was with me the whole time helping. I have never heard this song in the grocery store before and it did not come on ever again.

Today, a visit to the cemetery
and your spirit moved on.
A song came out of no where
to tell me of your joy.

When I went to pick out a place for my father's earthly remains, a plot was available right by his brother who he loved dearly. The chances of this were slim but the most interesting part was the way the plots appeared. My uncle lived right across the street from my father at an angle. These plots were exactly the same way. The messages continued to be clearly there.

The night light on the wall in the den where my mother always sat would just flicker continuously. Male spirits often come in this way. The first time I took notice to this was when my mom and I were watching the Kentucky Derby. This was an event that my parents always went together to watch. During the races, the light would not stop flickering. It continued until shortly after the race was over. I could feel my father's presence. I spoke to him and asked if he could make the light stop and then flicker three times. To my amazement, the light did this. When I moved to my house, he continued to flicker the lamp in my living room. One time, the light flickered on in the middle of the night as I got up to get something. I checked the bulb and everything about it. There was nothing wrong with the bulb or the lamp.

A Sign from Dad

Lights flicker to
my delight.
Tonight the lights
flicker with Dad's
new spirit life.

My parents grandfather clock had stopped working. I tried very hard to wind the clock so it would work. I remember my father coming home from physical rehabilitation for Thanksgiving and Christmas. He was able to get it to work but said "I think it may not work anymore but don't worry." Well, it stopped working after my father died. I tried to get it to work but it was completely dead. The next morning I heard the clock chime and my mother saying "The clock is working." I came out and looked at the clock in amazement. I knew my father had something to do with this. My father loved to fix and repair things. The night before, I heard these little noises like something rolling on the floor but couldn't see or find anything. I strongly felt my father's presence. The next day the clock started chiming.

On Valentine's Day my parents saw each other while my father was in the rehabilitation unit. They were like kids smiling and sharing some time together. My mother and I gave dad a small rose plant. I also gave my mother one. After my father crossed, this plant died completely. I could not think of throwing it out. It just had too much meaning behind it. So, I kept it on the window sill. Then one day, it bloomed the most beautiful single baby rose. It was bright red with very green leaves. Right away I knew my father had sent it to us. My mother smiled commenting that she was going to throw it out because it was dead. My mother was so happy that she kept the plant and it brought her some happiness. Every Valentine's Day always reminds me of the love my parents have for each other which is eternal.

My father's dear friend and golf buddy, Don Greico, sent me a letter. It was a beautiful letter with a picture of a cherry blossom tree. The golf course owners and Don planted this tree on the golf course. His friend had it planted at the beginning of the golf course to symbolizes the beginning; not the end. His comments on the funeral online stated that they would be golfing in Heaven. I believe this with all my heart. The companionship between them made golfing special. The tree reminds me that once we have completed our lessons, we travel back to our real home called Heaven. The tree symbolizes new beginnings and eternal life. Human physical death is not the end. It is a reminder to me that we will all reach our growth some day and transition back to be reunited with our loved ones on the other plane. Human physical death is not to be feared at all. It is to embrace with celebration when our time comes.

Myrtle Beach Golf Trips.

One day, I could not find the original picture used at my father's funeral of him in his uniform taken during the Korean War. It was in a plastic covered bag with a copy of a picture I made for a relative. The copied picture was of my father in his uniform and with my grandfather. I had it in the car under the American flag given to my mother at his funeral. The flap had gone back by accident so I thought it went under the seats. I looked for this while cleaning the car out. I had magazines in the back of the car. I went through every single magazine and item in the car. However, I could not find the picture. I later asked my father to send me a sign that he is still around me. Several weeks later, I went to the back of the car to get something out and the picture I had been looking for was sitting right on top of all the magazines.

Synchronized events continued to happen. The best example of this was when I was trying to sell my car so I could keep my father's immaculate vehicle. I had gone to the dealership twice but didn't like the offer. However, I did not try to get more money. I was feeling overwhelmed with so many things at the time. Then late on the evening of Mother's Day, something very interesting happened. My parents started helping with the sell of the car. I kept forgetting to get gasoline and at this point was near empty. I finally stopped to get gasoline when I discovered that my gas tank would not open. I really tried to open this but it would not budge. I had no choice but to go home and call for help. As I went home, I could feel my parents presence very strongly.

The next day, the dealership told me that there was a free tow because my car was new and under warranty. So, I scheduled a tow for my car. The guy came and within a few minutes had the gas tank open. I asked him to close it again but it was back to being stuck. He opened and closed the gas tank several times and then I asked him to leave it open so I could get gasoline. I wanted it towed and to have the dealership look at it. However, the tow place told me that they had to try to get it open first. So, I filled it with gasoline and went to the dealership anyway because I didn't want this to happen again.

As I sat in the waiting room, several interesting events happened. First, the person greeting me was very comforting. He did not know at this point that both of my parents had died. He later came out and told me that they could not find anything wrong with the gas tank or the lock. Everything worked perfectly fine. They would do the check up on the vehicle while there. As I waited, the lady who sold the car appeared. She passed by asking if I was waiting for her. I told her what happened and she told me I was in good hands with the repair shop. About 20 minutes later she walked by again and asked me if I still wanted to sell the car. She told me to just name the price of how much I wanted. So, I did and she came back a few minutes later asking about the title. She came close to the price but I wanted the price offered. Well, I got what I wanted and they were willing to come to my house to get the title. I thought to myself, could this really be happening? At the time, I did not think the title was with me. I also had to go to work to conduct a spirituality group. The dealership would mail the check to me once they received the title. The guy who came with me and helped clean out the car had also lost his mother right around the same time of my mother's crossing. I kept looking for the title but all along it was in my car.

When I bought the car which was right before my father's diagnosis, I gave the title to my father. My father gave it back to me and told me to put it temporarily in my car until I had my new file cabinet for it. I got side tracked with what happened with my father so it stayed in my car. I signed the title as I felt my father's presence and gave it to this guy to take to the dealership. Later, I called the dealership to let them know the car was coming back soon with the title. I wanted to know how long it would be before the check was ready. The person answering the phone happened to be the one who would take care of this. She told me the check would be ready soon and that is what happened. I found out later that the lady selling me the car had lost three family members in a short period of time several years ago. Also, the person greeting me when I brought the car in had experienced a loss. They all knew at one point about my parents crossing. Everything went so smoothly and I know that these events were set up to get the car sold. Thank you mom and dad from the bottom of my heart were the thoughts on my mind.

After my car was sold, I was able to start using my father's vehicle. When I first started using his car, the radio suddenly just stopped. A Frank Sinatra compact disc came on and started playing. I had no idea that this was still in the car. My uncle had searched all over to get this compact disc for my parents. It had a very special song on it that my father could not find anywhere. This is the song that started playing on the compact disc even though it is not the first song indicated to come on. The other thing that would happen and still does; the radio will just suddenly switch channels. Once the channel changed, a song would come on from my father. There is one song in particular that my father really loved and it has come on while leaving the cemetery. Also, this song comes on when finishing something connected to my father.

Don't take my faith away.
Death is transformation.
We travel back HOME
and become ONE eternally.

I had worked late one night and pulled up at my parents' house to get something. All of a sudden I smelled eggs cooking. I looked all around trying to find where the smell came from. I had not eaten and was so hungry. My father always had a meal left over and would cook eggs when he wasn't sure what to cook. Another message from my father, letting me know he was around and to get myself something to eat for dinner. My father was always kind, gentle, and wanting to offer a meal. We talked about many things over a bowl of soup. Soup was one of his favorites. Of course, my father would remind me to eat. I laughed out loud thinking to myself about this new spirit relationship with my dear father.

Oh, Lord, thank you for this new spirit relationship. Love never dies.

It seemed like the right people would show up at certain times even with my clients. I started to get many people grieving the loss of a loved one. I was not sure about being ready to process grief with others at this time. However, the referrals just kept coming and some of the situations were like a calling to do this. In one situation, the client's mother loses her husband and sister around the same time. It actually helped me with my own grief in some ways. Giving to others continued through the illness and crossing of my parents. I did not take a lot of time away from work. There were only brief periods away and then just balancing it out more.

The time with my clients was valuable in many ways. There was a little girl who had a lot of family problems and one day an angel appeared to her in my waiting room. The angel was described as blue with no face. I had seen a white orb near a lamp in the waiting room just before the session. Later after the session while talking with her mother, the little girl excitedly said "I have to tell you something." She then talked about the angel and when she looked back over her shoulder, the angel was gone. I can tell you that my father had been visiting me at this time while I was at the practice. I would hear noises of someone being present but no human being would be there. My clients at times even commented on this while in session with me. It was always comforting and reminded me of the times my father would stop by to say hello. He would offer to help out with many things including little repairs.

There was another teen who was struggling with family issues and she started to connect with the Lord. During a family session, the teen had a spiritual awakening. Her parents started to return to church. While we were discussing the Lord, she started to see hearts on the wood in my practice. I actually saw them too. In one particular area by my desk, she pointed out the face of Christ. We sat there in such amazement and delight. There was such a peaceful and comforting feeling. It was if the room was full of pure love.

Thank you dear client for the honor of serving you. This time has been a special journey.

One evening I asked my father to send me some specific messages. I ask my father to please let me know that I will see him in Heaven. Please send me something like a clear message in the sky or maybe just write it on the computer. Then I laughed and said out loud that this would be asking too much. Within a few days my father would send some incredible messages to me.

My lap top had not been working for several months. I went to buy a mouse attachment and tried to get it to work. However, it still was not working. I turned the computer on and off a few times trying to get it to work. Suddenly the computer worked and so did the writing across the computer. It clearly said "Dad" in big bold letters on the blue background. I just kept looking at this in total amazement. It was like looking at the sky with writing that looked like a cloud. The letters were very distinct and clearly said "Dad" and then there was this "E" close near the end. Of course, our last name starts with an "E". Also, it stayed on my computer lap top. I decided to take a picture of this which is shown below. Of course I am not doing this to prove anything. This book is not about proving any of the messages received. I just couldn't resist taking the picture because I had something that was still there. The orb in the photograph covered part of the writing but you can clearly see the large "D". My computer suddenly crashed later and I was unable to take another picture. I don't think it would of made a difference because my dad is represented as the orb which covers the other letters in the photograph.

The next day, I hear a chime at 1:00 am and then whistling while on the computer. My father was trying to get my attention. He did whistle while doing some things. The whistling came from above my right shoulder while at the computer reading. My father always enjoyed reading a good book. I could feel his presence all night long. It was interesting because I was reading material about the metaphysical world.

During this next visitation, my father makes himself known and my dog goes crazy barking. My dog only barks when she hears an animal, door bell, and for good reason. She does not bark at anything. This went on for awhile and then my dog just stopped. My father was letting me know that he was there to visit. I could strongly feel his presence and the room was so full of pure love.

Every time something difficult would arise in dealing with the systems when you lose a loved one; my father would let me know he was near by sending a special song or several Beatles songs. One time I was having a hard time with the systems after my parents crossing. A very special song about life after death came on from the Beatles. I knew my parents were both close by helping me. It was so touching that tears of happiness came to my eyes.

This next event happened while at home. I was really missing my father and started cleaning through many items. As I am going through old magazines to give away, I found a puzzle that my father completed. My father loved doing these puzzles. In the middle of the puzzle, the word love was there. I found this puzzle at a time when I was thinking of my father and remembering how much I love him. He had written love in the middle of the puzzle as part of figuring it out. The message was so clear to me that he was sending his love and letting me know that love is the key. My father's love for me is eternal. Love is the one thing that does not die.

Some interesting events occurred with my father's sisters during the summer. First, his oldest sister falls and hits her head. She goes to the emergency room and seems to be alright. She fell sometime in late June. Then his next oldest sister seems to take a possible fall but gets admitted as a heart patient. Shortly after this happens, his youngest sister takes a fall and ends up in the heart unit. My father seem to want me to visit his sisters and revealed this in my dreams. Then I felt my father's presence wanting me to visit his youngest sister who he was closest to. She had taken a fall right before the celebration of my father's birthday and mine. I ended up seeing her the day after our birthday. It was too hard to go there on my birthday due to being in the same hospital and unit last July with my mother before she crossed. I was not sure initially what this all meant but later realized my father's presence when my aunt told me how much she loved me.

"Mirror Reflections"

Words are powerful
Yet sometimes painful
Other times just so pure

No running for me
Empower me

Light my way
As I light yours
No running away, the time is near
Energy so pure
Brighten my light, lead the way
I am here
Closer then you know
Feel your way
Be ready for love
As the time draws near

Our souls evolve and grow more as
The Universe calls
Two souls reunite as One
Galaxies far and near
I AM HERE...

My parents' house needed some repairs as time moved ahead. I had contacted some contractors to get some estimates but none of these contractors seem to work out. Then there was this one contractor that came to do an estimate. While in the basement with this contractor, a golf ball came rolling out on the floor near my father's golf clubs. I picked it up and felt his presence. Then the contractor asked me again about the walls ever being drywalled. I knew the walls were waterproofed before at least once and maybe twice. However, I was not sure when the waterproofing took place. I told this contractor that sometimes my father gives answers. This was when the golf ball actually rolled out of no where and I felt this urge to go over by his work bench. This is where I found one empty can of drywall. My father had answered the contractor's question. I can still remember his face when all this happened. He was able to get the date off the paint can and had a good idea as to when the basement was waterproofed. I knew without a doubt that this was the right contractor to hire and he did a very nice job.

On the anniversary month of my mother's crossing, I stopped to get something to drink. The young woman acted as if she knew me. It took me a few minutes and then I realized that it was a volunteer that was with us at times during my mother's stay in the intensive care unit. She asked how my mother was doing and I gave her the news. She looked very sad and I told her that my mother just traveled back to where she belongs. Of course, she was looking a little puzzled. I told her to just look for my book about the messages. She eagerly indicated interest in doing this.

There was only a slim chance of me running into this volunteer a year later on the anniversary of my mother's crossing. This was definitely no coincidence. She remembered us so well and wanted to know how my mother was doing. I remember her kindness by the concern she showed at the hospital and at this very moment in time. Another synchronized event had occurred during this journey called grief. This event would let me know that everything would be alright. My mother's presence could be felt very strongly and there was just a blessed feeling of love.

The synchronized events would continue on this journey of grief. One day I went to get a ring guard for a pinky ring that my father had given to me for my birthday. The ring kept slipping off and I wanted to make sure a new guard was put on to protect it. While in the jewelry store, this beautiful sparkling butterfly was just looking at me. The message from my mother was clear. So, I bought the butterfly and knew my parents were there with me. It was the best feeling ever. It was like they were rejoiced at me getting the ring guard and the butterfly. There was an overall sense of joy and excitement.

More incredible events would continue to guide me on this journey. One night I went to turn over and actually felt the blanket go up in the air and over me to cover me up. I felt these feather like touches around my face and knew my mother was comforting me. This happened during a time of my grief when my sleeping patterns where not the best which many people go through on their journey with grief. The message of eternal love would continue on this journey.

"Eternal Soul"

Many flowers appear
Orchids, peonies, hibiscus
Among a few to name
Sweet fragrances of memories
Many moons and galaxies away
Exist now and forever
In a place of no time or space
Intoxicating sweet fragrances
Embrace you once again
So many life times to name in the journey
So long and yet so short
With no space or time
Blue and red salvinas
All around with daffodils and lilies
But most of all orange blossoms appear
Loving imperfections and all
Dreaming again as
Eternal love returns from the deepest blue seas.

My father was very adamant about this picture over my television. From time to time, this picture would be crooked for no apparent reason. Later, I would connect the messages that my father would be sending to me. Sometimes he would do this to let me know he was still around and other times a specific message. He was also great at turning the television off and letting me know that I needed to be working on some special projects. My father wanted me to tell the world about Heaven. My mother was part of this too. A large glass angel that my mother bought me somehow came off the stereo and landed on the front of a chair while I was on the phone. The large angel was glass but didn't break. This happened twice and a small clock with an attached angel kept falling too.

During my later journey of grief, the Lord brought me closer and closer to him. I was brought forth to Eucharistic Adoration. The church in our area opened an Adoration Chapel. I began to enjoy my weekly time in the Adoration Chapel. One day I went with a friend but not during my normal hour. A woman there approached me and asked if I saw red writing on the host. I really looked but did not see anything. I decided when it was my holy hour of time, I would look for the writing described by her. My time came and the first thing I did was to look for the writing. However, no writing appeared.

While in prayer, I started to see a face. It was faded at first and then became brighter and glowing. I was seeing the face of Christ. Before this happened, I was praying the divine mercy chaplet and playing the music tune for this. I asked the Lord to give me a specific message about something. The next "adorer" came in and she could see the face of Christ too. We took some pictures which did surprisingly come out to some degree. Some people could see the face of Christ in person and others could not. This was true for the printed photographs too. We both hugged in rejoice of this vision. I was so at peace and yet excited at the same time. I went back before my hourly time and the Lord's face was still there. His face appeared right after Ash Wednesday and the entire time of lent. This was my second blessing in seeing the Lord's face. A true miracle that brought so much inner peace. The Lord has carried me on this journey of grief. I am now able to place my feet down walking again with guidance and love.

Untouched photographs of Christ appearing.

This brings me to Palm Sunday morning after both of my parents had crossed over. I was partially awake but trying to fall back to sleep. During this time, I heard my mother in her normal morning routine. She came to visit me in the most glowing beautiful light three times early this same morning.

Palm Sunday was always a special time of year for my mother. I didn't understand this in quite the same way as I do now. This is the time of year the Lord promises us eternal life by dying for all of us. I embraced this beautiful light and hugged my mother. I could feel her from the other side. My mom came to tell me that she never really left and was with me this special day. She lets me know that there is life after death. I hold on to these special blessings from the Lord. I think of this experience and others when my journey with grief gets difficult. I believe truly that having faith after all that has happened, gives me these special moments and new relationship with my family.

"Guided by my Angels"

The gorgeous sunset came
Rainbow colors all around
Being in one dimension
Seeing the beautiful sunset
Yet being in another plane with a rainbow
Just seem to join together as ONE
Seeing an Angel
As the Angel wings wrapped around me
Hearing the whispered message
Go with your intuition
Your child imagination
Believe it!
Feel it and Play it out
Your soul knows
Your inner child remembers
Just ask, predestined
The Angels are lining up
All in the Divine name
There is no time
All in the nothingness
Turning around
Hearing ocean waves
Special desire appears
Heart pounding fast
Known this all along
The other part of my soul joins
My inner child looks up and smiles
Heaven on earth as ONE.

I use to think about retirement as my future because this is the way our society is set up but I have always been different. My mother asked me what I would eventually do before she crossed. She thought perhaps I would retire and go back to Florida. I could not even think about life without my mother. It was already so difficult without my father being around. I live much more by the day now. I have no retirement plans. Besides, I plan on helping many more people by working in my field destined for me as part of fulfilling my purpose on earth. I can't even imagine not serving others. I do not know what tomorrow brings and focus only on the present moment. God already has a plan for me and he knows the ending. The journey of grief made me grow in many ways as I embraced grief. I am where I need to be on my path. A part of me yearns to be in the other world called Heaven. I think of traveling back home to eternal divine love and light in God's Kingdom. Right now, I will continue to serve others and fulfill my purpose here on earth. This is what we all need to do until it is our time.

While reviewing pictures I had taken inside my parents' house and some of the memorial stone at the cemetery, I would find messages. Some had white orbs and one picture had angels over it. This was the same room where I saw an angel and the face of Christ. This picture was actually of some horses hanging on the wall. However, on the photograph printed, there are visible angels. The photograph looks very different from the actual picture. This photograph does not show the color or horses clearly. There seem to be many angels around my parents' house.

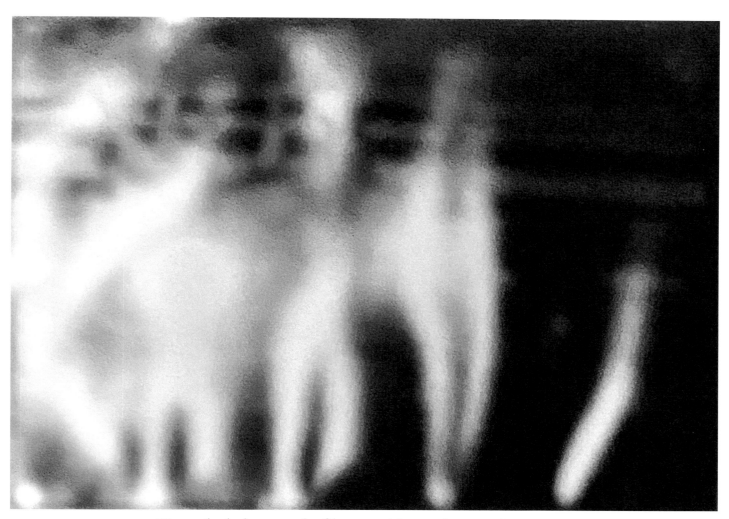

Untouched photograph of horses with *angels* appearing over it.

After both of my parents went to Heaven, I would start to see a particular red cardinal every year outside my large picture window. Sometimes the red cardinal would be with his mate. He would peek in my window saying hello. One year on the anniversary of my father's death, the red cardinal appeared looking at me. I recall this being a time when there was something going on and I was wishing for my father to be here with me. For sure, my father would visit me to let me know that everything would be alright. Sometimes both cardinals would appear to let me know that my parents are in Heaven together in their new spirit bodies. My mother loved birds and it would be just like her to send my father to say hello. It would also make sense that she would pop in briefly to send her love but not stay long. My mother would want me to have that special time with my father.

"Red Cardinal Blessing"

Little red cardinal peeking in my window...
A gift from Heaven sending blessings of bliss
while dancing on the branches and joining his
mate...messages from beyond saying, we are
ONE in eternal love...

If you don't already know, there is a battle going on involving our souls. I can't even remember how many times I have felt this darkness . During my grief, there were terrible episodes but the Lord was there. I will refer to these episodes as journey of the dark soul. During this time, I was so blessed to see the face of Christ which brought me to the bright light. I had to learn to balance the light and dark even more so during this journey with grief, just like when the sunsets graciously allowing the moon to shine at night. The ying and yang of balancing our own energies is most important. We all have our shadows to face in this life time and physical death of our loved ones is challenging.

As I grew closer to the Lord during my grief, the darkness became more vivid then ever. So terribly dark that I have to admit death felt like it was near. My faith was truly tested many times. The darkness was so manipulating and cunning that I can remember a few times of feeling as though I was almost dead myself. There came a time when the Lord actually picked me up and started carrying me. There is no other explanation as to how I stayed alive with my health deteriorating. I realized that I would remain here for a purpose. The purpose would be to continue serving and helping people. In particular, there would be some major future events that would impact the world. I would continue to help people with mental health issues as well as grief during these times. I would reach a very large number of people through finally publishing these writings and more which would include poems never published.

There are some important messages to summarize from my beloved parents. First, you will see all your loved ones again in a pure white light of vibrational energy. There will be a feeling of being completely at home in Heaven with so much pure love. There will be a feeling of being completely at Home with so much love. Our bodies will be in a spirit form that gives us eternal life. Until your time comes, remember to laugh a lot, co-create what you want in the present moment with focused intention and make the best of every moment. You can have Heaven on earth if you remember to implement these things. Most of all, be grateful each day and master the art of living in the present moment. Earth is full of lessons and illusions which help us to evolve and return home to Heaven as ONE. It is important to learn how to embrace the dark to evolve and balance our energies.

As I end this series of "Dying to Live," I open my eyes and realize the Lord has blessed me in a time of deepest sorrow with the gifts of miracles, visions, prophecies and the greatest gift of all.......Eternal Love.

I have written many poems over the years. This includes all the poems in this book. I want to dedicate this particular poem called "Souls by the Seashore" to my beloved parents. Mostly because they met on Miami Beach and they are still together as ONE in Heaven. The ying and yang of balance as a couple on earth...now infinite love.

"Souls by the Seashore"

Find me by the seashore
Where the white sand glows
Star fish and shells
Seagulls all around
By the seashore tide
Sand dollars wash around
While peaceful doves appear
Footprints are there
Dancing in the sand
Where my heart has always been
Find me by the seashore
With dolphins all around
Ocean waves, low tides, seaweed on the side
Salt water smell
Sail boats all around
Feel me in the air
My soul has always been there
With no one around
Eyes will not see me
You will feel me though
Come join me
By the seashore playing in the sand
where my heart has always been
Our souls join in
As doves fly again.

Mom meets dad in Miami Beach at Haulover Beach.

Dad and me in Miami Beach at South Beach.

Thousand Islands Boat Cruise

In Loving Memory of Reiki

7/29/2002-9/17/2017

Since the writing of this book, Reiki crossed over to Heaven and was reunited with my beloved parents at the Rainbow Bridge. She was my companion dog for over 16 years and a therapy dog who helped many people. She participated in the local dog shows and was awarded ribbons. Reiki also received special acknowledgment for being a therapeutic service dog. Reiki is now a special *angel* in Heaven

Brief Biography of the Author:

The author of this book is a native of Florida. She was raised during her early childhood years in Miami and lived in Tampa Bay for many years. She currently resides in Lee, New York. She also has several degrees in the area of psychology, clinical social work, criminology and criminal justice. In addition, she has several special certifications in her field of expertise including trauma and clay therapy for children. She is a licensed psychotherapist in private practice with psychotherapy privileges (R #) in Upstate New York area. She has the highest credential standing in her state and national recognition as a Board Certified Diplomat with the American Board in Clinical Social Work.

Many people over the years have described her as creative and gifted. She describes herself as an energy therapist and knowing her purpose in this world. She also has been described as a master soul. Her experience in mental health and addictions is extensive. She has practiced licensed for over 20 years and been in the field for well over this time. She specializes in trauma and anxiety. Other areas of expertise are relationships, domestic violence and youth at risk. She has worked as a intuitive healer and Reiki Master for over 25 years. She utilizes color light therapy and emotional freedom techniques as two of her many clinical interventions. She has written online articles about codependency and is part of a online therapy practice which serves people all over the world.

The author is well known for her spiritual leadership and dedication to helping people. She developed her practice called Sacred Heart Healing Center and combined it with healing the mind, body, and spirit. The Lord guided her from a young child when her family moved from Florida to New York. A situation occurred that later in life would connect her to the healing field. She received a message from the Lord guiding her with the name of her practice which many people have been drawn to. "I am thankful for my gifts which are from the Lord and my dear parents who departed to Heaven in 2011." She believes that Grace gives us our gifts to use while we are here on earth experiencing a human existence and that we are all here to learn about love. She has already started "Dying to Live," Part II Series, sharing powerful messages from both of her parents who have reunited in Heaven as infinite love. The continued Sacred journey with grief from Heaven to earth.

Printed in the United States
by Baker & Taylor Publisher Services